Critical Th[illegible] Detective™

Vocabulary

Book 2

Critical Thinking Detective™ series is available in print or eBook form.

Beginning • Book 1 • Book 2

Math Beginning • Math

Vocabulary Book 1 • Vocabulary Book 2

Written by
Diane Hartsig

Edited by
Patricia Gray

Graphic Design by
Scott Slyter

THE CRITICAL THINKING CO.™
www.CriticalThinking.com
Phone: 800-458-4849 • Fax: 541-756-1758
1991 Sherman Ave., Suite 200 • North Bend • OR 97459
ISBN 978-1-60144-949-8

Printed in China by Shanghai Chenxi Printing Co., Ltd. (June 2021)

Table of Contents

About the Author

Diane Hartsig earned a journalism degree from Michigan State University and an elementary education degree from Western Michigan University. She has nine years of teaching experience and is currently a fifth-grade teacher. Diane is passionate about promoting children's acquisition and usage of language. She is the author of *Critical Thinking Detective, Vocabulary Book 1* and *2* and *Vocabulary Riddles—A - Z Catastrophes Book 1* and 2. She lives in Dowagiac, Michigan with her husband and has three children.

About This Book

Vocabulary is a key component of this collection of fun mysteries for Grades 5-12 and *Book 2* incorporates all-new words from *Book 1*. The vocabulary in this book was gathered from a multitude of sources including SAT/ACT word lists and the author's reading selections. The *Merriam-Webster.com Dictionary* provided many of the vocabulary details including usage, look-up popularity, synonyms, and antonyms.

Each activity features between 18 and 24 vocabulary words and every one of them has the potential to implicate or exonerate a suspect. Solving the mysteries requires the reader to evaluate vocabulary words and to analyze and synthesize pieces of information. Critical thinking improves as students assess evidence found through reading comprehension and deductive and inductive thinking skills.

After solving each case, the second part of the activity gives versatility to the vocabulary words as students practice using them in a different context. Readers choose the appropriate word from the word list to complete each sentence. When the word lists contain synonyms, students have flexibility in their choices.

These activities and their vocabulary words are not easy, but don't despair. If you take the time to decipher the unknown words and reread, you'll have sharper critical thinking skills and an expanded vocabulary.

How to Solve These Cases

- Read each activity carefully and keep in mind that all statements are true.
- Each activity establishes two to three parameters to identify the culprit. Consider the parameters as you evaluate the statements from the suspects and witnesses. Drawing a picture is helpful.
- Remember that every vocabulary word is important to solve each case. Consult a dictionary as needed for definitions and pronunciations.
- As you look up words, be aware which are synonyms and antonyms of each other.
- Make notes when you find evidence. Synthesizing more than one piece of evidence can often establish innocence or guilt.
- Use the process of elimination to narrow down each list of suspects.

Read the case below to find evidence to identify the innocent and guilty suspects. Remember, the story and suspects' statements are true.

The Thieving Blatherskite

[1]Earlier this year, authorities in Fenton investigated the Thieving Blatherskite—a thief who stole an expensive dress from Fenton's Finery. [2]Three sales associates described the thief as a disheveled customer, whose incessant clattering caused agitation with the staff.

[3]The information from employees narrowed the list of culprits to the four suspects shown below. [4]After further questioning, one suspect confessed, and police discovered the dress among her chattels later that day.

Sales Associate #1: [5]"I have worked for the store for a long time and know the suspects well. [6]Leila Haskins is notable for her badinage and Ann Peterson for her pell-mell mien. [7]On the day of the theft, I had an immersing conversation with Ella Madison before Petra Cummins interjected."

Sales Associate #2: [8]"My shift was just beginning when the thief stole the dress. [9]I overheard my peeved cohorts griping about Ann Peterson and Petra Cummins—the latter for being taciturn."

Sales Associate #3: [10]"When she's in the store, Ella Madison commandeers my attention. [11]I have worked exclusively with the natty customer for the past year. [12]She is a pertinacious but loyal customer."

Ann Peterson

Leila Haskins

Ella Madison

Petra Cummins

Based on the evidence, circle the Thieving Blatherskite.

After solving the case, write the best vocabulary word to complete each sentence. Each word can only be used once.

mien	natty	peeved	cohorts	interject
badinage	chattels	clattering	incessantly	taciturn
finery	disheveled	immersing	pertinacious	
agitation	gripe	pell-mell	commandeered	

1. The leaky faucet dripped ____________________ all night.
2. The ____________________ witness was reluctant to answer questions.
3. Speak louder so I can hear you over the group's ____________________.
4. I had a/an ____________________ appearance after the windy walk.
5. The protestors' ____________________ delayed the start of the project.
6. During an emergency, supplies can be ____________________ by authorities.
7. My ____________________ was on display during the black-tie event.
8. We were in a hurry, so we packed in a/an ____________________ manner.
9. The bedroom is too small to contain my ____________________.
10. The conversation's flow will be smoother if you don't ____________________.
11. The ____________________ in the program have similar backgrounds.
12. To discourage their ____________________, the teacher moved the friends apart.
13. The first chapter is dull, but the rest of the book is ____________________.
14. I entered the makeover contest to improve my ____________________.
15. In anticipation of the promotion, I invested in a/an ____________________ wardrobe.

Read the case below to find evidence to identify the innocent and guilty suspects. Remember, the story and suspects' statements are true.

The Disruptive Denizen

[1]On October 7 of this year, police investigated the Disruptive Denizen. [2]Over several months, the denizen's neighbors made multiple complaints of plangent noise in the densely-populated neighborhood, but they were unsure of the noise's source. [3]Investigators canvassed local households and narrowed their search to a row of four houses radiating away from the city center.

[4]Police interviewed the occupants of the four houses, and their statements appear below. [5]One suspect admitted to the noise, but denied any cognizance of its disruption to the neighborhood. [6]Nevertheless, police cited the denizen for violating the city's noise ordinance.

Millie Linton

[7]"My abode is closest to downtown and I savor the amenities. [8]The cacophony is part of the experience, so I don't understand why one person should be singled out."

Jane Dalton

[9]"Several of my friends live in the neighborhood and, at their urging, I moved here for a more convivial experience. [10]Initially, the neighbors extended a cordial welcome."

Camille Turner

[11]"Coming from downtown, my domicile is the penultimate house in the row. [12]I know who the denizen is—her yard flanks mine."

Mae Hanson

[13]"I have lived conterminous to Millie for six months now. [14]Even though I revel in throwing large soirees, I go to great lengths to be a solicitous neighbor."

Based on the evidence, circle the Disruptive Denizen.

After solving the case, write the best vocabulary word to complete each sentence. Each word can only be used once.

cognizance	nevertheless	ordinance	cacophony	domicile
flanks	soiree	amenity	denizen	radiated
savored	abode	cordial	plangent	
conterminous	convivial	penultimate	canvass	

1. To lure buyers, the condominium offered ____________________, such as a pool and workout room.
2. The campaign sought to raise people's ____________________ about endangered species.
3. California and Nevada are ____________________ states.
4. The group split up, so they could ____________________ more people.
5. Your ____________________ should reflect your personal style.
6. Debris ____________________ from the center of the crater.
7. The ____________________ featured an impressive guest list.
8. The council adopted a/an ____________________ to preserve the city's historical features.
9. The alarm clock's ____________________ woke the drowsy student.
10. The organization recruited members through ____________________ invitations.
11. After the promotion, the employee ____________________ the accompanying perks.
12. The property owner evicted the ____________________ from the property.
13. I was disappointed to receive my ____________________ choice for classes.
14. At dinner, my new acquaintances were ____________________.
15. The southern edge of the park ____________________ my property.

Read the case below to find evidence to identify the innocent and guilty suspects. Remember, the story and suspects' statements are true.

The Pernicious Polluter

[1]Recently, authorities in Odenville investigated a polluter who contaminated a local stream by perniciously dumping construction waste. [2]The only witness to the crime was an angler who frequents the spot at dusk. [3]He reported seeing a conspicuously-marked truck with a lone driver backing up by the stream. [4]The witness recognized the truck's ubiquitous carmine logo, but could not identify the company.

[5]Based on the witness's account, authorities correctly inferred the polluter represented a salient local company. [6]They interviewed several workers from active construction sites in the area. [7]After the interviews, police arrested one of the suspects and his subsequent confession incriminated the company's owner.

Calvin Dodson

[8]"For 20 years I've worked in construction. [9]Recently, I took a supervisor job for an inchoate company. [10]Our trucks are bereft of insignias."

Ben Lawrence

[11]"My employer has a well-known rubicund emblem and a multitude of employees. [12]They always work in tandem in manifold roles."

Jonathon Liggins

[13]"Occasionally, my employer asks me to make deliveries. [14]I have no contrition over the iniquitous ways the company addresses its debris."

Alex Davidson

[15]"I'm a driver for a notable company with a viridescent trademark. [16]My duties include picking up orders, as well as dropping off refuse for disposal."

Based on the evidence, circle the Pernicious Polluter.

After solving the case, write the best vocabulary word to complete each sentence. Each word can only be used once.

emblem	inchoate	refuse	contrition	manifold
notable	pernicious	conspicuous	incriminate	ubiquitous
viridescent	carmine	insignia	tandem	
bereft	iniquitous	salient	debris	

1. The author's first draft represented the ______________________ version of the idea.

2. Newspapers publish lists of ______________________ books for children.

3. In spring, the landscape becomes ______________________.

4. The editors worked in ______________________ to publish the book.

5. The stark room was ______________________ of warmth.

6. The chemical is only ______________________ if you fail to follow the directions.

7. Citing a lack of ______________________, the judge refused the suspect's bail.

8. I placed the keys in a/an ____________________ place I could easily see.

9. The flooding victims heaped _________________________ by the curb.

10. The student's ______________________ behavior led to expulsion.

11. To generate a new ______________________, the school sponsored a design competition.

12. The ______________________ song saturated the airwaves.

13. The multi-talented performer accepted ___________________ projects.

14. The class decorated their _____________________ cards for Valentine's Day.

15. The prosecutor used eye-witness testimony to _____________________ the defendant.

Read the case below to find evidence to identify the innocent and guilty suspects. Remember, the story and suspects' statements are true.

The Prevaricator

[1]In October, authorities in Kent County solved a theft at a home improvement store. [2]Several bystanders witnessed the crime and gave statements to the police.

[3]According to the official report, a corpulent thief entered the store alone and circled the perimeter of the store several times in a clockwise pattern. [4]He examined several hand drills in a cursory manner before concealing one with his raiment. [5]He left the store through an appurtenant exit.

[6]The information from the bystanders was invaluable to solving the crime, but one statement was incongruous to the rest. [7]It complicated the investigation, and led authorities to charge the witness with prevaricating a statement to the police. [8]The witnesses and their statements appear below.

Sebastian Reyna

[9]"My statement was a compendious account of the theft. [10]The replete thief was standing next to me as he slipped the hand drill under his toggeries."

Curtis Evans

[11]"The thief passed me as he circled the store in a deasil pattern. [12]I saw him steal the drill and leave through the peripheral exit. [13]The statement I provided to the police contained infallible information."

Rony Naser

[14]"I didn't see the thief slip the drill into his vestments. [15]But, as I included in my statement, I did see his helter-skelter examination of the drills. [16]It was clear he was ensconcing something as he left through the auxiliary exit."

Carter Chavez

[17]"I explained to the police how the thief circled the store in a widdershins manner before he slipped the drill into his valise."

Based on the evidence, circle the Prevaricator.

After solving the case, write the best vocabulary word to complete each sentence. Each word can only be used once.

compendious	toggeries	ensconced	deasil
incongruous	cursory	prevaricate	peripheral
replete	invaluable	auxiliary	vestments
corpulent	valise	helter-skelter	
infallible	appurtenant	raiments	

1. Once I found the missing book, the series was ______________________.
2. The traveler's ______________________ was too large to carry on the plane.
3. The chemistry tutoring was ______________________ to improving my grade.
4. A/an ______________________ reading of the draft will not catch all the mistakes.
5. The political candidate with a fraudulent diploma ______________________ to the public
6. As the project grew, staff needed ______________________ places to work.
7. The documentary contained shocking but ______________________ information.
8. I ______________________ some candy in my purse to enjoy during the movie.
9. While we played the game, we took turns in ______________________ order.
10. The teacher marked the research paper down for its ______________________ information.
11. Large meals during the holidays leave me feeling ______________________.
12. The small closets in old houses are not ideal for modern ______________________.
13. The larger-than-expected crowd needed ______________________ seating.
14. I take some of my finer ______________________ to the dry cleaners.
15. You can use the attic for ______________________ storage.

Read the case below to find evidence to identify the innocent and guilty suspects. Remember, the story and suspects' statements are true.

The Trying Troglodyte

[1]In May, the human resource department at Claringten Bank received complaints about the Trying Troglodyte—an employee who affronted co-workers by promulgating outmoded ideas. [2]The troglodyte was known for voraciously defending her convictions, which often exacerbated the situation. [3]The social breaches typically happened during lulls in the workday and with employees of lesser eminence than the troglodyte.

[4]The human resource department interviewed several employees to identify the offending employee. [5]Once identified, the department offered additional training in workplace etiquette, which the troglodyte grudgingly accepted.

Employee #1: [6]"I've had contretemps with Florence Wickman before. [7]Her provincial ideas have always been the cynosure of our discord. [8]Katherine Kline and Ava Pope are the preponderant members of the group."

Employee #2: [9]"Katherine Kline and Ava Pope staunchly bulwark their persuasions. [10]Katherine Kline's viewpoints are superannuated, especially compared to Ava Pope's."

Employee #3: [11]"Ava Pope is well-known for having tête-à-têtes with co-workers during respites in the workday. [12]They are never in front of Abigail Henshaw, who is noteworthy for her probity."

Katherine Kline

Ava Pope

Abigail Henshaw

Florence Wickman

Based on the evidence, circle the Trying Troglodyte.

After solving the case, write the best vocabulary word to complete each sentence. Each word can only be used once.

eminence	grudgingly	staunchly	affront	exacerbated
probity	respite	cynosure	etiquette	provincial
tête-à-tête	contretemps	preponderant	promulgated	
bulwark	outmoded	superannuated	breach	

1. The town constructed a sea wall to ________________________ waterfront homes.

2. I updated my music collection by purging ________________________ songs.

3. After working so much, I felt entitled to a/an ________________________.

4. The harsh ointment ________________________ the irritation of the skin.

5. In college, medieval art was my ________________________.

6. When I needed career advice, I scheduled a/an ________________________ with my mentor.

7. I ________________________ some business leaders by not consulting them on the economic policy.

8. Winning the award increased my ________________________ as an artist.

9. The school gives citizenship awards to recognize outstanding ________________________.

10. My viewpoints seemed ________________________ when I moved to Chicago.

11. Signed first editions are the ________________________ books in my library.

12. To avoid ________________________, the host banned discussions of politics.

13. The company ________________________ the finalists for the managerial job.

14. The environmental activists were ________________________ against the destruction rainforests.

15. Entering without knocking is a/an ________________________ of privacy.

Read the case below to find evidence to identify the innocent and guilty suspects. Remember, the story and suspects' statements are true.

The Insolent Impostor

[1]The Insolent Impostor was an uninvited guest to a recent Saturday night charity auction. [2]The event—which raised money for indigent citizens—catered to well-heeled leaders of the Port Huron Community. [3]After insolently entering the event, the impostor cast numerous bids on a hodge-podge of valuable items, which he later reneged on.

[4]The impostor had idiosyncrasies which police used to identify him. [5]He chortled assuredly between bids and was quite risible. [6]Attendees of the event described the impostor as charismatic and were dumbfounded by his duplicity.

[7]The impostor's unfulfilled bids kept the charity from reaching its mark. [8]Once he was identified, the impostor agreed to pay a portion of his bids. [9]The items were then reauctioned to recoup costs and attain the charity's goal.

Charles Lemont

[10]"I attended the auction for indisposed members of my community. [11]Although I cast numerous bids, none of my endeavors came to fruition."

Jamal Harrison

[12]"As a responsible member of my community, I participate in charitable auctions, but my bids reflect my tastes which are quite explicit. [13]Two things stood out at Saturday night's auction: William Dow's erudition and Leon Sevren's guffaws."

William Dow

[14]"I am coy at auctions, but I enjoy them unless Charles Lemont is there. [15]He is always cagey with his bids."

Leon Sevren

[16]"On Saturday, several people commented on my drollness. [17]It was an indelible evening."

Based on the evidence, circle the Insolent Impostor.

After solving the case, write the best vocabulary word to complete each sentence. Each word can only be used once.

cagey	fruition	idiosyncrasies	dumbfounded	hodge-podge
explicit	insolent	attain	guffaw	well-heeled
indisposed	assuredly	erudition	recoup	
coy	endeavor	indigent	duplicity	

1. The student was pleased with her paper and handed it to me ________________________.
2. On the night of the party, the planning came to________________________.
3. When you complete the list, be ________________________ in the details.
4. The substitute filled in for me while I was ________________________.
5. Small claims court will help you ________________________ what you lost.
6. The lawyer's defense strategy rested on the expert's ________________________.
7. Only ________________________ philanthropists have buildings named after them.
8. My aversion to pink is just one of my ________________________.
9. We were admitted into the competitive program after our third ________________________.
10. The ________________________ collection lacked a unifying theme.
11. Sponsors helped ________________________ kids attend the summer camp.
12. I was ________________________ by the mechanic's outrageous bill.
13. In a/an ________________________ move, the employee asked for a substantial raise.
14. The ________________________ customer was reluctant to sign the contract.
15. The ________________________ was heard throughout the quiet library.

Read the case below to find evidence to identify the innocent and guilty suspects. Remember, the story and suspects' statements are true.

The Malingering Manager

[1]Recently, employees at a production company in Marshall complained about the Malingering Manager. [2]The company's owner frequently extoled and rewarded the manager for successfully executing elaborate projects. [3]The owner was oblivious to the manager's chronic malingering and delegation of duties to her underlings. [4]Employees classified all dealings with the manager as curt and derisory, which added to their feelings of being unappreciated and unvalued.

[5]To identify the malingerer, the owner interviewed four employees. [6]Once identified, the malingering manager accepted a reassignment and a diminishment in pay and duties.

Employee #1: [7]"I often correspond with Alice Linden and Carolyn Mailer. [8]Communication with these managers is pithy."

Employee #2: [9]"Carolyn Mailer is a neophyte and only works on elemental projects. [10]I work a lot with Hannah Pine and Alice Linden. [11]I have to disregard the pejorative tone of one of them to keep the project on track."

Employee #3: [12]"All of my projects have been with Fatima Antar. [13]Working with her is a delectation. [14]Any allocation of duties is apt for the situation."

Employee #4: [15]"I work a lot with Hannah Pine and Alice Linden to different corollaries. [16]Hannah increases my aplomb, and Alice my incumbencies."

Alice Linden

Hannah Pine

Fatima Antar

Carolyn Mailer

Based on the evidence, circle the Malingering Manager.

After solving the case, write the best vocabulary word to complete each sentence. Each word can only be used once.

corollary	elaborate	elemental	apt	derisory
diminishment	pejorative	aplomb	delegate	malingered
neophyte	allocation	delectation	incumbency	
correspond	curt	extol	chronic	

1. To make the schedule more realistic, I had to ______________________ some tasks.
2. After a month of a/an ________________________ cough, I finally went to the doctor.
3. Technology makes it easier to ________________________ with friends.
4. Everyone received the same amount, so the _______________________ was fair.
5. My appointment to the library board was quite ________________________, given my background.
6. The _______________________ in attendance caused the museum to close.
7. The teacher's encouragement strengthened the child's ______________________.
8. The _______________________ challenged the established firm's practices.
9. When it was time for school, the child often _______________________.
10. The _______________________ response consisted of one word.
11. The complicated design was edited to create a/an ______________________ version.
12. The _______________________ comments eroded morale.
13. Adopting a rescue dog was a/an ________________________ I didn't foresee.
14. I occasionally indulge in the ______________________ of eating chocolate.
15. Flunking the test was a/an _______________________ of not studying.

Read the case below to find evidence to identify the innocent and guilty suspects. Remember, the story and suspects' statements are true.

The Careless Curator

[1]In April, the board at the Belvedere History Museum reviewed complaints about the Careless Curator. [2]His transgressions included indolence and dereliction. [3]Fellow employees said the curator was refractory. [4]Inaccuracies that were pointed out to him received only remonstrant dismissals followed by languid corrections.

[5]Worried about the integrity of the museum, the board interviewed the museum's four curators. [6]The Careless Curator admitted to having subpar criterion. [7]He expressed disapproval of the museum and was summarily dismissed from his position.

Edwin Balfour

[8]"My credentials are impeccable, and I adhere to the loftiest canons in my curation. [9]I've consulted with John Wilhelm for exhibits. [10]He acquiesces to admonitions."

John Wilhelm

[11]"I am relatively new to the museum and think of Eric Deron as my mentor. [12]I suggest emendations that receive dilatory responses."

Eric Deron

[13]"Exhibits at this museum seem to be an aggregate of all the curators. [14]I give all of the curators' suggestions the demur I believe they deserve."

Kyle Rafferty

[15]"With the most experience of anyone here, I consider myself the de facto head curator. [16]We peer review each other's exhibits and my colleagues have noted my alacrity."

Based on the evidence, circle the Careless Curator.

After solving the case, write the best vocabulary word to complete each sentence. Each word can only be used once.

acquiesced	demur	loftiest	canon	indolence
de facto	languid	alacrity	emendation	summarily
integrity	aggregate	dilatory	subpar	
admonition	dereliction	mentor	credential	

1. I threw out the first batch of cookies for being ____________________________.
2. People who repeatedly lie have no ____________________________.
3. The paper printed a/an ____________________________ after publishing the wrong date for the festival.
4. The struggling parent didn't appreciate the ____________________________ from strangers.
5. The employee's ____________________________ kept her from being promoted.
6. The group project needed contributors with ____________________________.
7. I was assigned a/an ____________________________ during my first year at the firm.
8. After our supervisor abruptly resigned, I became the ____________________________ leader.
9. Attending the selective college fulfilled one of my ____________________________ goals.
10. I went ahead with the project despite the ____________________________.
11. The group ____________________________ to the proposal after we made some changes.
12. After grandmother fainted, we ____________________________ called an ambulance.
13. The collage was a/an ____________________________ of different mediums.
14. The double shift caused the intern to be ____________________________.
15. The computer certification was the only ____________________________ I lacked.

Read the case below to find evidence to identify the innocent and guilty suspects. Remember, the story and suspects' statements are true.

The Emphatic Editor

[1]Recently, the owner of a large publishing company in Chicago heard complaints about the Emphatic Editor. [2]The company's writers correctly inferred the editor was spending too little time mulling over submissions. [3]The writers avoided the editor for her emphatic, but adverse suggestions. [4]They claimed any revisions handled by the editor would distort their message and diminish the merit of their work.

[5]The company's owner interviewed four writers who were outspoken about their perspectives. [6]When the Emphatic Editor was identified, the owner counselled her on the value of constructive discourse. [7]The editor remained on the publishing team under the watchful eye of the owner.

Writer #1: [8]"Carmen Alvarez gives assertive feedback. [9]Her suggestions are apropos to my writing, while Olivia Hinton's are attenuating."

Writer #2: [10]"Elena Garcia peruses any writing given to her. [11]Lately, I've worked with Charlotte Benz. [12]Her ardent suggestions augment my writing."

Writer #3: [13]"I just finished a large project with Olivia Hinton. [14]Her suggestions were succinct and resounding."

Writer #4: [15]"More often than not, I work with Elena Garcia. [16]She can be vehement about her sagacious suggestions."

Carmen Alvarez

Elena Garcia

Olivia Hinton

Charlotte Benz

Based on the evidence, circle the Emphatic Editor.

After solving the case, write the best vocabulary word to complete each sentence. Each word can only be used once.

adverse	counselled	revisions	attenuating	mull
constructive	resounding	assertive	merit	vehement
perused	ardent	emphatic	succinct	
apropos	discourse	sagacious	augment	

1. I did additional research to ______________________ the paper's thesis.
2. The additional illustrations in the book were ______________________ to the theme.
3. I ______________________ the car's manual to diagnose the problem.
4. When the band broke up, they wrote a letter to their most ______________________ fans.
5. The pharmacist ______________________ me on the side effects of my prescription.
6. The committee designed the survey to gather ______________________ feedback.
7. The ______________________ weather conditions made an outdoor party unlikely.
8. I consulted the senior members of my firm for ______________________ career advice.
9. After the lecture, I continued the ______________________ with the guest speaker.
10. The raise and promotion are a testament to your ______________________.
11. I replied with a/an ______________________ no, but the salesperson continued to call.
12. Please gather the feedback and assemble a/an ______________________ compilation.
13. You need to ______________________ over the proposal before you decide anything.
14. Reading is a/an ______________________ factor for cognitive decline.
15. I only signed the contract after acceptable ______________________ were made.

Read the case below to find evidence to identify the innocent and guilty suspects. Remember, the story and suspects' statements are true.

The Jackleg Carpenter

[1]In September—during the culmination of a pivotal project—the owner of Lansworth Construction explored complaints of shoddy workmanship. [2]The work belonged to the Jackleg Carpenter who was only hired through an act of nepotism by the site manager. [3]The carpenter had been at the site since the inception of the project in May and flaunted his favoritism. [4]His co-workers loathed him for his deportment.

[5]To get the project back on track and maintain his reputation, the owner interviewed four carpenters on the project. [6]During the interview, the inaptness of one carpenter became apparent and he was terminated from the company.

Eric Rodriguez
[7]"My co-workers are sentient of my affiliation with management, but it's my incondite work they regard."

Sam Linwood
[8]"I joined the project at its nascence. [9]I have only worked with Martin Flores once, but I mention his work with approbation."

Martin Flores
[10]"It's quite common to be hired through a liaison. [11]Sam Linwood remits his relationship while Eric Rodriguez vaunts his."

Sean Avery
[12]"During this project, I've developed amity with the crew. [13]My crackerjack work distinguishes me from the other carpenters."

Based on the evidence, circle the Jackleg Carpenter.

After solving the case, write the best vocabulary word to complete each sentence. Each word can only be used once.

amity	jackleg	remitted	culmination	liaisons
distinguished	pivotal	crackerjack	incondite	vaunted
nascence	approbation	inception	terminate	
apparent	inaptness	sentient	deportment	

1. The failing company ____________________ its bills.
2. Our ____________________ returned after we worked out our disagreement.
3. My high SAT scores ____________________ me from the other college applicants.
4. The ____________________ bridge had to be replaced after several years.
5. The award and ____________________ boosted my confidence.
6. If your ____________________ is unacceptable, you will be asked to leave.
7. After the couple won the lottery, they ____________________ their newfound wealth.
8. Showing at the famous museum was the ____________________ of my career.
9. The ____________________ lawyer reduced his client's sentence to time served.
10. Your dishonesty becomes ____________________ when you can't keep your story straight.
11. The wiring by the ____________________ electrician wasn't up to code.
12. Americans abroad depend on embassies as ____________________ to the government.
13. I couldn't put the book down during the ____________________ point in the plot.
14. Very young children can be ____________________ of their surroundings.
15. Investors in Amazon during its ____________________ are very wealthy.

Read the case below to find evidence to identify the innocent and guilty suspects. Remember, the story and suspects' statements are true.

The Fluent Finagler

[1]Midland Police recently investigated the case of a saleswoman who went door-to-door peddling discount lawn services to homeowners. [2]The saleswoman—who was described as fluent and affable—answered questions with postulated diligence. [3]She cultivated and accepted cash down payments and ostensibly scheduled the service for the following month. [4]When the homeowners realized they had been finagled, the saleswoman was long gone.

[5]Midland Police worked with neighboring law enforcement to create a list of four potential suspects. [6]Interviews with the suspects' clients—shown below—allowed police to identify the Fluent Finagler. [7]She was charged and ultimately convicted of her crimes.

Client #1: [8]"Lilah Tumah is known for guileless business propositions and answering questions with imperiousness."

Client #2: [9]"Hanna Storm is well-suited for sales, because she is both articulate and amiable. [10]During her sales pitch, she gave cash down payments her imprimatur."

Client #3: [11]"I let Adele Francis in for a gauche sales pitch after I saw her at my neighbor's house. [12]She talked for about half an hour and was dulcet the entire time."

Client #4: [13]"Genial Elizabeth Pearl has a proscription concerning cash down payments. [14]She is eloquent and amenable to answer questions."

Lilah Tumah

Hanna Storm

Adele Francis

Elizabeth Pearl

Based on the evidence, circle the Fluent Finagler.

After solving the case, write the best vocabulary word to complete each sentence. Each word can only be used once.

amenable	fluent	peddled	diligence	imperiousness
finagle	ostensibly	cultivate	guileless	ultimately
imprimatur	articulate	genial	proscription	
amiable	gauche	postulated	eloquent	

1. The unprepared and nervous speaker gave a/an ____________________ presentation.
2. The most __________________________ people will dedicate their lives to social causes.
3. You can _________________________ friendships by asking people about their interests.
4. To raise money for the field trip, students ________________________ magazine subscriptions.
5. ________________________ people have a wide circle of friends.
6. I admire the _________________________ it takes to earn a doctorate degree.
7. The _________________________ representative clearly outlined the organization's goals.
8. After the philanthropist's death, her entire estate _______________________ went to charities.
9. The beauty product became more fashionable after the celebrity's _____________________.
10. I practiced my speech several times to be more _________________________.
11. The two candidates had equal qualifications, so we hired the more _____________________ one.
12. It is difficult to accept a/an __________________________ theory without any evidence.
13. The principle looked for a/an __________________________ witness to interview about the incident.
14. The __________________________ on loud car stereos made the neighborhood more peaceful.
15. After his promotion, our former co-worker looked at us with _________________________.

Read the case below to find evidence to identify the innocent and guilty suspects. Remember, the story and suspects' statements are true.

The Bellicose Hoarder

[1]In January, the owner of Hamlin Apartments suspected one of his four tenants of hoarding. [2]According to the apartments' manager, the hoarder was bellicose with neighbors and referred to his staggering amount of junk as a "collection." [3]The "collection" was concordant in nature, and was tenaciously gathered over a long period of time. [4]The hoarder offered no pretexts for his behavior.

[5]To identify the hoarder, the owner interviewed the building's four tenants. [6]Once identified, the hoarder was given—based on safety concerns—an ultimatum: [7]cleanup his property or be evicted from the premises.

Ethan Grover

[8]"I have a prodigious collection which I have sporadically amassed over time. [9]I keep to myself here, especially after the contention with my raffish neighbor—Ken Heywood.

Augustine Mandova

[10]"For five years now, I have lived with pugnacious neighbors—Ethan Grover and Simon White. [11]They have accumulated portentous collections."

Simon White

[12]"I pursue my collection with doggedness. [13]Unlike Augustine Mandova, I cull my items based on their coherency.

Ken Heywood

[14]"My sundry collection was assembled over time. [15]No one in this apartment complex fathoms my fealty."

Based on the evidence, circle the Bellicose Hoarder.

After solving the case, write the best vocabulary word to complete each sentence. Each word can only be used once.

amassed	fathom	sporadically	contention	prodigious
doggedness	raffish	concordant	pretexts	ultimatum
pugnacious	coherency	premises	tenaciously	
bellicose	portentous	sundry	culled	

1. The parents resorted to a/an ________________________ to get the child to cooperate.

2. The professor accepted no ________________________ for missing assignments.

3. From her collection, I ________________________ the best photos for the collage.

4. The teammates' ________________________ helped them regain the lead.

5. The author's books focus on one ________________________ theme.

6. It is ________________________ to wear a hat while you're eating dinner.

7. The ________________________ group represented the various cultures in the neighborhood.

8. It was difficult to reach an agreement with the ____________________ group member.

9. I couldn't ________________________ the confusing explanation.

10. Every American should enjoy the ________________________ views of the Grand Canyon.

11. After the department was downsized, its policies became ______________________ enforced.

12. Their ________________________ was so loud, we could hear them through the closed door.

13. The restraining order would not allow the suspect near the ________________________.

14. I practiced my free throw shot until I reached a high level of ________________________.

15. I booked the multi-country tour based on its ________________________ opportunities.

Answers

The Thieving Blatherskite (pages 2-3)

The Innocent

Leila Haskins: From sentence 2, the thief agitates the staff with clattering. In sentence 6, Haskins is notable for her badinage. This eliminates Leila Haskins.

Ella Madison: Employees describe the thief as disheveled in sentence 2, but Madison is natty in sentence 11. In sentence 2, incessant clattering agitates the staff. Madison is having an immersing conversation in sentence 7. This eliminates Ella Madison.

Petra Cummins: In sentence 2, the thief incessantly clatters. Cummins is taciturn in sentence 9. This eliminates Petra Cummins.

The Thieving Blatherskite

Ann Peterson is the Thieving Blatherskite because the process of elimination exonerates the other suspects. From sentence 4, we know one suspect confessed and had the dress among her chattels. In sentence 2, the thief is described as disheveled. Peterson's mien is described as pell-mell in sentence 6. In sentence 2, the thief is agitating the staff. Employees are griping about Peterson in sentence 9.

1. incessantly
2. taciturn
3. clattering
4. disheveled or pell-mell
5. agitation
6. commandeered
7. finery
8. disheveled or pell-mell
9. chattels
10. interject
11. cohorts
12. badinage
13. immersing
14. mien
15. natty

Vocabulary Words and Appropriate Synonym for Context Within Case

Vocabulary Word	Synonym
agitation	uproar
badinage	playful banter
blatherskite	one who talks nonsense
chattels	belongings
clattering	noisy talk
cohorts	associates
commandeered	seized
disheveled	lacking order
finery	dressy clothing
gripe	complain
immersing	interesting
incessantly	constantly
interject	interrupt
mien	appearance
natty	sharply dressed
peeved	annoyed
pell-mell	sloppy
pertinacious	stubborn
taciturn	closedmouthed

The Disruptive Denizen (pages 4-5)

Millie Linton

Jane Dalton

Camille Turner

Mae Hanson

The Innocent

Millie Linton: Sentence 11 states that Camille Turner's property is the penultimate, or third in the row of four houses. According to sentence 12, the denizen's yard flanks Turner's property, which puts the denizen in the second or fourth house. In sentence 7, Linton's house is closest to town, which puts her in the first house. This proves Millie Linton's innocence.

Camille Turner: In sentence 12, Turner says the denizen's house flanks her property. This proves Camille Turner's innocence.

Mae Hanson: In sentence 2, the neighbors are filing complaints with the police over the plangent noise. From sentence 14, we know Hanson goes to great lengths to be a solicitous neighbor. This proves Mae Hanson's innocence.

The Disruptive Denizen

Jane Dalton is the Disruptive Denizen by using a process of elimination, which exonerates the other suspects. From sentences 5 and 6, we know that one suspect confessed and received a citation from the police. Dalton mentions in sentence 10 that "initially" her neighbors were cordial, which implies they aren't as friendly anymore. There is no other evidence proving that Jane Dalton is not the Disruptive Denizen.

1. amenities
2. cognizance
3. conterminous
4. canvass
5. abode or domicile
6. radiated
7. soiree
8. ordinance
9. cacophony
10. convivial or cordial
11. savored
12. denizen
13. penultimate
14. convivial or cordial
15. flanks

Vocabulary Words and Appropriate Synonym for Context Within Case
The Pernicious Polluter (pages 6-7)

Vocabulary Word	Synonym
abode	home
amenity	advantage
cacophony	loud noise
canvass	question
cite	call to appear in court
cognizance	awareness
conterminous	having a common boundary
convivial	social
cordial	friendly
denizen	resident
domicile	home
flank	border
nevertheless	even so
ordinance	a public regulation
penultimate	next to last
plangent	loud
radiate	proceeding in a line
revel	enjoy
savor	enjoy
soiree	party
solicitous	thoughtful

The Innocent

Calvin Dodson: In sentence 5, the polluter represents a salient company. Sentence 9 describes Dodson's company as inchoate. The witness describes the polluter's truck as conspicuously marked in sentence 3. In sentence 10, Dodson describes his trucks as bereft of insignias. This exonerates Calvin Dodson.

Ben Lawrence: From sentence 3, we know the polluter was alone. In sentence 12, workers in Lawrence's company always work in tandem. This exonerates Ben Lawrence.

Alex Davidson: The polluter's truck has a carmine logo in sentence 4. In sentence 15, Davidson's company has a viridescent trademark. This exonerates Alex Davidson.

The Pernicious Polluter

Jonathon Liggins is the Pernicious Polluter. We know police arrested one of the workers who later confessed from sentence 7. A process of elimination has exonerated the other suspects. In sentence 14, he feels no contrition and he labels his company's actions as iniquitous.

1. inchoate
2. notable or salient
3. viridescent
4. tandem
5. bereft
6. pernicious
7. contrition
8. conspicuous
9. debris or refuse
10. iniquitous
11. insignia or emblem
12. ubiquitous
13. manifold
14. carmine
15. incriminate

Vocabulary Words and Appropriate Synonym for Context Within Case

The Prevaricator (pages 8-9)

Vocabulary Word	Synonym
bereft	lacking
carmine	red
conspicuous	obvious
contrition	regret
debris	garbage
emblem	symbol
inchoate	just beginning
iniquitous	morally wrong
insignia	symbol
incriminate	imply guilt
manifold	various
notable	well-known
pernicious	harmful
refuse	waste
rubicund	red
salient	well-known
tandem	together
ubiquitous	being everywhere
viridescent	green

Sebastian Reyna

Curtis Evans

Rony Naser

Carter Chavez

The Innocent

Sebastian Reyna: In sentence 3, the thief is described as corpulent. Reyna describes him as replete in sentence 10. The thief slips the drill in his raiment in sentence 4, and Reyna says he slips the drill under his toggeries in sentence 10. This eliminates Sebastian Reyna.

Curtis Evans: The thief circles in a clockwise pattern and leaves through an appurtenant exit in sentences 3 and 5. In sentences 11 and 12, Evans reports how the thief passed him in a deasil pattern and leaves through the peripheral exit. He calls his report infallible in sentence 13. This eliminates Curtis Evans.

Rony Naser: In sentence 4, the thief examines the drills in a cursory manner. In sentence 15, Naser calls the thief's examination helter-skelter. The thief leaves through an appurtenant exit in sentence 5. In sentence 16, Naser sees the thief leave through an auxiliary exit. This eliminates Rony Naser.

The Prevaricator

Carter Chavez is the Prevaricator because the process of elimination exonerates the other suspects. From sentence 7, we know police charged a witness with prevaricating a statement. In sentence 3, the thief is circling in a clockwise pattern. Chavez reports the thief circling in a widdershins pattern in sentence 17. The thief slips the drill into his raiment in sentence 4, but in sentence 17, Chavez says the thief uses his valise.

1. compendious
2. valise
3. invaluable
4. cursory or helter-skelter
5. prevaricated
6. appurtenant, auxiliary, or peripheral
7. infallible
8. ensconced
9. deasil
10. incongruous
11. corpulent or replete
12. raiments, toggeries, or vestments
13. appurtenant, auxiliary, or peripheral
14. raiments, toggeries, or vestments
15. appurtenant, auxiliary, or peripheral

Vocabulary Words and Appropriate Synonym for Context Within Case

Vocabulary Word	Synonym
appurtenant	supplemental
auxiliary	supplemental
compendious	complete
corpulent	fat
cursory	hasty
deasil	clockwise
ensconce	conceal
helter-skelter	hasty
incongruous	incorrect
infallible	true
invaluable	key
peripheral	supplement
prevaricate	lie
raiments	clothing
replete	overweight
toggeries	clothes
valise	small suitcase
vestments	clothing
widdershins	counterclockwise

The Trying Troglodyte (pages 10-11)

Katherine Kline

Ava Pope

Abigail Henshaw

Florence Wickman

The Innocent

Florence Wickman: From sentence 1, we know the troglodyte affronts co-workers with outmoded ideas. In sentence 7, Wickman's ideas are provincial. This eliminates Florence Wickman.

Ava Pope: The troglodyte affronts co-workers and voraciously defends her convictions in sentences 1 and 2. In sentence 11, Pope is interacting with co-workers in tête-à-têtes. This eliminates Ava Pope.

Abigail Henshaw: In sentence 1, the troglodyte affronts co-workers, but in sentence 12, Henshaw is noteworthy for her probity. This eliminates Abigail Henshaw.

The Trying Troglodyte

Katherine Kline is the Trying Troglodyte because a process of elimination exonerates the other suspects. From sentence 5, we know the troglodyte was identified and accepted additional training. In sentence 1, we know the troglodyte affronts co-workers with outmoded ideals. In sentence 10, Kline's beliefs are superannuated. The troglodyte voraciously defends her convictions in sentence 2, and Kline staunchly bulwarks her persuasions in sentence 9. Lastly, from sentence 3, we know the troglodyte's social breaches happened with co-workers of lesser eminence. In sentence 8, Kline is a preponderant member of the group.

1. bulwark
2. outmoded or superannuated
3. respite
4. exacerbated
5. cynosure
6. tête-à-tête
7. affronted
8. eminence
9. probity or etiquette
10. provincial
11. preponderant
12. contretemps
13. promulgated
14. staunchly
15. breach

Vocabulary Words and Appropriate Synonym for Context Within Case

Vocabulary Word	Synonym
affront	offend
breach	violation
bulwark	safeguard
contretemps	disagreement
conviction	belief
cynosure	focus
discord	division
eminence	notability
etiquette	manners
exacerbate	worsen
grudgingly	reluctantly
lull	pause
outmoded	out-of-date
persuasions	set of beliefs
preponderant	notable
probity	character
promulgate	announce
provincial	small-town
respite	rest
staunchly	devotedly
superannuated	out-of-date
tête-à-tête	one-on-one
troglodyte	old-fashioned person
trying	difficult

The Insolent Impostor (pages 12-13)

Charles Lemont

Jamal Harrison

William Do

Leon Sevren

The Innocent

Charles Lemont: From sentence 2, we know the impostor attended an auction for indigent citizens. Lemont attended an auction for indisposed citizens in sentence 10. This eliminates Charlene Lemont.

Jamal Harrison: In sentence 3, the impostor bids on a hodge-podge of items. Harrison's bids reflect his explicit taste in sentence 12. This eliminates Jamal Harrison.

William Dow: The impostor is risible and charismatic in sentences 5 and 6. Dow describes himself as coy in sentence 14. This eliminates William Dow.

The Insolent Impostor

Leon Sevren is the Insolent Impostor. From sentence 8, we know police identified the impostor and he agreed to pay a portion of his bids. A process of elimination exonerates the other suspects. In sentence 5, the impostor chortles between bids. Harrison comments on Sevren's guffaws in sentence 13. The impostor is risible in sentence 5. In sentence 16, auction attendees comment on Sevren's drollness.

1. assuredly
2. fruition
3. explicit
4. indisposed
5. recoup
6. erudition
7. well-heeled
8. idiosyncrasies
9. endeavor
10. hodge-podge
11. indigent
12. dumbfounded
13. insolent
14. cagey
15. guffaw

Vocabulary Words and Appropriate Synonym for Context Within Case

Vocabulary Word	Synonym
assuredly	confidently
attain	reach
cagey	cautious
charismatic	charming
chortle	to laugh
coy	shy
dumbfounded	shocked
duplicity	deception
drollness	humor
endeavor	attempt
erudition	knowledge
explicit	specific
fruition	completion
guffaw	laugh
hodge-podge	assortment
idiosyncrasy	quirk
indelible	memorable
indigent	needy
indisposed	sick
insolent	bold
recoup	regain
renege	to back out
risible	funny
well-heeled	rich

The Malingering Manager (pages 14-15)

Alice Linden

Hannah Pine

Fatima Antar

Carolyn Mailer

The Innocent

Hannah Pine: From sentence 4, we know the Malingering Manager makes employees feel unvalued. In sentence 16, Pine increases the employee's aplomb. This eliminates Hannah Pine.

Fatima Antar: In sentence 3, the manager is chronically malingering and delegating duties. Employee #3 calls Antar's allocation of duties apt in sentence 14. In sentence 4, dealings with the offending manager are derisory, but in sentence 13, dealing with Antar is a delectation. This eliminates Fatima Antar.

Carolyn Mailer: In sentence 2, the Malingering Manager is working on elaborate projects. Mailer only works on elemental projects in sentence 9. This eliminates Carolyn Mailer.

The Malingering Manager

Alice Linden is the Malingering Manager. A process of elimination exonerates the other suspects. From sentence 6, we know the owner identified the Malingering Manager. In sentences 4 and 5, dealings with the Malingering Manager are curt and derisory. In sentence 8, communications with Linden are pithy. In sentence 11, she is named as one of two possible managers with a pejorative tone. From sentence 3, we know the Malingering Manager delegates duties. In sentence 16, Linden is increasing Employee #4's incumbencies.

1. delegate
2. chronic
3. correspond
4. allocation
5. apt
6. diminishment
7. aplomb
8. neophyte
9. malingered
10. curt
11. elemental
12. derisory or pejorative
13. incumbency
14. delectation
15. corollary

Vocabulary Words and Appropriate Synonym for Context Within Case

Vocabulary Word	Synonym
allocation	distribution
aplomb	confidence
apt	appropriate
chronic	habitual
corollary	effect
correspond	communicate
curt	brief
delectation	delight
delegate	assign
derisory	belittling
diminishment	reduction
elaborate	complex
elemental	simple
extol	praise
incumbency	responsibility
malinger	to pretend or exaggerate illness to avoid work
neophyte	newcomer
oblivious	unaware
pejorative	demeaning
pithy	short and meaningful
underling	one with less power

The Careless Curator (pages 16-17)

Edwin Balfour

John Wilhelm

Eric Deron

Kyle Rafferty

The Innocent

Edwin Balfour: In sentence 6, the Careless Curator has subpar criterion. From sentence 8, we know Balfour has the loftiest canons. This eliminates Edwin Balfour.

John Wilhelm: The Careless Curator is refractory in sentence 3, but Wilhelm acquiesces to admonitions in sentence 10. This eliminates John Wilhelm.

Kyle Rafferty: In sentence 3, the Careless Curator is refractory. The other curators note Rafferty's alacrity in sentence 16. This eliminates Kyle Rafferty.

The Careless Curator

Eric Deron is the Careless Curator because the process of elimination exonerates the other suspects. From sentence 7, we know one of the curators was dismissed for being the Careless Curator. In sentence 4, we know the Careless Curator had languid corrections to inaccuracies. In sentence 12, Deron had dilatory responses to emendations. In sentence 4, the Careless Curator responded to inaccuracies with remonstrant dismissals. Deron gives the curators' suggestions demur in sentence 14.

1. subpar
2. integrity
3. emendation
4. admonition
5. dereliction or indolence
6. alacrity
7. mentor
8. de facto
9. loftiest
10. demur
11. acquiesced
12. summarily
13. aggregate
14. dilatory or languid
15. credential

Vocabulary Words and Appropriate Synonym for Context Within Case

Vocabulary Word	Synonym
acquiesce	agree
admonition	advice
aggregate	collection
alacrity	willingness
canon	conduct
credential	qualification
criterion	standard
curator	a collection supervisor
de facto	in effect but not recognized
demur	protest
dereliction	intentional neglect
dilatory	slow
emendation	correction
impeccable	flawless
indolence	laziness
integrity	truthfulness
languid	slow
loftiest	highest
mentor	a trusted guide
refractory	resistant
remonstrant	protesting
subpar	unacceptable
summarily	without delay
transgression	offense

The Emphatic Editor (pages 18-19)

Carmen Alvarez

Elena Garcia

Olivia Hinton

Charlotte Benz

The Innocent

Charlotte Benz: In sentence 3, we learn the Emphatic Editor's suggestions are adverse for the writers' work. From sentence 12, we know Benz's suggestions augment the writing. This eliminates Charlotte Benz.

Elena Garcia: In sentence 2, the editor doesn't take enough time to mull over the writers' submissions. Garcia peruses the writing in sentence 10. From sentence 3, we know the editor's suggestions are adverse for the writers' work. In sentence 16, Garcia's suggestions are sagacious. This eliminates Elena Garcia.

Carmen Alvarez: From sentences 3 and 4, we know the editor is giving adverse suggestions and distorting the meaning of the writers' work. In sentence 9, Alvarez's suggestions are apropos to the writing. This eliminates Carmen Alvarez.

The Emphatic Editor

Olivia Hinton is the Emphatic Editor. A process of elimination exonerates the other suspects. From sentence 6, we know the company's owner identified the Emphatic Editor. In sentence 4, we know the editor is diminishing the merit of the writers' work. Hinton's suggestions are called attenuating in sentence 9. The editor gives emphatic suggestions in sentence 3. Hinton's suggestions are resounding in sentence 14.

1. augment
2. apropos
3. perused
4. ardent
5. counselled
6. constructive or sagacious
7. adverse
8. constructive or sagacious
9. discourse
10. merit
11. assertive, emphatic, resounding, or vehement
12. succinct
13. mull
14. attenuating
15. revisions

Vocabulary Words and Appropriate Synonym for Context Within Case

Vocabulary Word	Synonym
adverse	unfavorable
apropos	relevant
ardent	emotional
assertive	pushy
attenuating	reducing
augment	build up
constructive	helpful
counsel	guide
distort	change
discourse	conversation
emphatic	forceful
merit	worth
mull	consider
outspoken	direct
perspective	viewpoint
peruse	read, typically thoroughly
resounding	forceful
revision	change
sagacious	insightful
succinct	to the point
vehement	forceful

The Jackleg Carpenter (pages 20-21)

Eric Rodriguez

Sam Linwood

Martin Flores

Sean Avery

The Innocent

Sam Linwood: In sentence 3, the Jackleg Carpenter flaunts his favoritism. Sam Linwood remits his relationship in sentence 11. This eliminates Sam Linwood.

Martin Flores: There are complaints of shoddy workmanship in sentence 1. In sentence 9, Sam Linwood has approbation for Flores' work. This eliminates Martin Flores.

Sean Avery: From sentence 4, we know the Jackleg Carpenter's co-workers loath him. In sentence 12, Sean Avery has amity with his crew. There are complaints of the Jackleg Carpenter's shoddy workmanship in sentence 1. In sentence 13, Avery's work is crackerjack. This eliminates Sean Avery.

The Jackleg Carpenter

Eric Rodriguez is the Jackleg Carpenter because the process of elimination exonerates the other suspects. From sentence 6, we know the Jackleg Carpenter's inaptness became apparent and he was terminated from the company. In sentence 1, there are complaints of shoddy workmanship from the Jackleg Carpenter. Rodriguez calls his own work incondite in sentence 7.

1. remitted
2. amity
3. distinguished
4. incondite
5. approbation
6. deportment
7. vaunted
8. culmination
9. crackerjack
10. apparent
11. jackleg
12. liaisons
13. pivotal
14. sentient
15. inception or nascence

Vocabulary Words and Appropriate Synonym for Context Within Case

Vocabulary Word	Synonym
affiliation	connection
amity	friendliness
apparent	clear
approbation	praise
crackerjack	exceptionally good
culmination	height
deportment	behavior
distinguish	separate
jackleg	amateur
inaptness	unfitness
inception	beginning
incondite	badly constructed
liaison	connection
loath	hate
nascence	beginning
nepotism	favoritism based on relationship
pivotal	critical
regard	consider
remit	ignore
sentient	aware
shoddy	inferior
terminate	end employment
vaunt	parade

The Fluent Finagler (pages 22-23)

Lilah Tumah

Hanna Storm

Adele Francis

Elizabeth Pearl

The Innocent

Lilah Tumah: From sentence 4, we know the homeowners were finagled. Tumah has guileless business propositions in sentence 8. This eliminates Lilah Tumah.

Adele Francis: In sentence 2, the finagler is fluent, but Francis gives a gauche sales pitch in sentence 11. This eliminates Adele Francis.

Elizabeth Pearl: The finagler cultivates and accepts cash down payments in sentence 3. Pearl has a proscription concerning cash down payments in sentence 13. This eliminates Elizabeth Pearl.

The Fluent Finagler

Hanna Storm is the Fluent Finagler because the process of elimination exonerates the other suspects. From sentence 6, we know police identified the finagler who was ultimately convicted of her crimes. In sentence 2, the finagler is described as fluent and affable. Storm is articulate and amiable in sentence 9. The finagler cultivates and accepts cash down payments in sentence 3. Storm gives cash down payments her imprimatur in sentence 10.

1. gauche
2. amenable
3. cultivate
4. peddled
5. amiable or genial
6. diligence
7. articulate, eloquent, or fluent
8. ultimately
9. imprimatur
10. articulate, eloquent, or fluent
11. amiable or genial
12. postulated
13. guileless
14. proscription
15. imperiousness

Vocabulary Words and Appropriate Synonym for Context Within Case

Vocabulary Word	Synonym
affable	pleasant
amenable	willing or open
amiable	pleasant
articulate	well-spoken
cultivate	encourage
diligence	commitment
dulcet	pleasant
eloquent	well-spoken
finagle	cheat or trick
fluent	well-spoken
gauche	awkward
genial	pleasant
guileless	honest
imperiousness	superiority
imprimatur	approval
ostensibly	seemingly
peddle	hawk
postulated	assumed
proscription	restriction
ultimately	eventually

The Bellicose Hoarder (pages 24-25)

Ethan Grover

Augustine Mandova

Simon White

Ken Heywood

The Innocent

Ethan Grover: From sentence 3, we know the hoarder tenaciously collected over time. Grover collects sporadically in sentence 8. This eliminates Ethan Grover.

Augustine Mandova: In sentence 3, the hoarder's collection is concordant. We know Mandova does not cull items based on their coherency from sentence 13. This eliminates Augustine Mandova.

Ken Heywood: The hoarder's collection is concordant in sentence 3. In sentence 14, Heywood's collection is sundry. This eliminates Ken Heywood.

The Bellicose Hoarder

Simon White is the Bellicose Hoarder because the process of elimination exonerates the other suspects. We know, from sentence 6, the hoarder was identified and received an ultimatum. In sentence 2, the hoarder is bellicose with neighbors. White is described as pugnacious in sentence 10. In sentence 3, the hoarder tenaciously collects. White collects with doggedness in sentence 12.

1. ultimatum
2. pretexts
3. culled or amassed
4. doggedness
5. concordant
6. raffish
7. sundry
8. bellicose or pugnacious
9. fathom
10. portentous or prodigious
11. sporadically
12. contention
13. premises
14. coherency
15. portentous or prodigious

Vocabulary Words and Appropriate Synonym for Context Within Case

Vocabulary Word	Synonym
amass	gather
bellicose	argumentative
coherency	consistency
concordant	consistent
contention	heated disagreement
cull	select
doggedness	persistence
fathom	understand
fealty	commitment
hoard	stockpile
portentous	staggering
premises	grounds
pretext	excuse
prodigious	amazing
pugnacious	argumentative
raffish	rude
sporadically	spottily
sundry	diverse
tenaciously	persistently
ultimatum	condition